A READER'S JOURNAL

Designed by Peggy Lauritsen Design Group

Printed on 50% & 100% recycled paper,
including a minimum of 10% post-consumer waste.

To order copies of this book,
or *A Young Reader's Journal,*
you may contact the publisher.
However, try your local book
or gift store first.

The Write Style
15111 Tammer Lane
Wayzata, MN 55391
612.476.7932

*In celebration of my daughter, Jessica,
her power, her voice and her dreams.*

A Note from the Publisher

At book club one night, a member of our group announced that she wanted to share something special with us. She produced two insignificant-looking, old notebooks, which indeed were old, but they certainly were not insignificant. These were two of her grandmother's reading logs.

With full understanding of the meaning of this awesome gift, we expressed admiration and curiously paged through entries to learn what kinds of books she read and what she thought. After a while, the others turned their attention to new topics and the delicious dessert offered by our host. However, like a blazing fire, the idea of a reader's journal burned in my mind. Why hadn't I thought of it? I wished I had started keeping my own when I was 15 years old. Wouldn't it be interesting to look back and to read what I thought when I first read books like *War and Peace, Native Son,* and *Marjorie Morningstar.* For a long time I could think of nothing else, so I searched the bookstores and gift shops. When I found nothing that I wanted to use, I resolved to publish one.

Romantic visions of rummaging through attic trunks, discovering readers' journals and getting to know someone through the books they chose to read and their ideas consumed me. With this vision and my belief in the power of the written idea, I worked with the talented graphic designers, Peggy Lauritsen and Michelle Solie, to create *A Reader's Journal* so that you and I would have a place where we feel comfortable and motivated to ponder and to express our thoughts. I hope it is a book you will enjoy filling with ideas, memorable quotes, lists of all those books you hope to read and whatever else comes to mind.

I created *A Reader's Journal* as a gift to myself, but I think it is the perfect gift for friends and family with whom I share many happy times talking about books. I hope you feel the same way. Perhaps, like my friend in book club, someone close to you will experience the extraordinary pleasure of discovering more about you through your reading journals.

Margie Shapiro

P.S. For a special young person in your life, consider A Young Reader's Journal, *designed to encourage reading and writing and to build self esteem through valuing one's own voice.*

Table Of Contents

Books, Books and More Books JOURNAL ENTRIES

TITLE ....

Author ....

Date .... Recommended by ....

Opinions/Ideas ....

....

....

....

....

....

....

....

....

....

....

....

....

....

....

....

....

....

TITLE

Author

Date **Recommended by**

Opinions/Ideas

TITLE ....

Author ....

Date .... Recommended by ....

Opinions/Ideas ....

....

....

....

....

....

....

....

....

....

....

....

....

....

....

....

....

....

....

....

....

TITLE ....

Author ....

Date .... Recommended by ....

Opinions/Ideas ....

....

....

....

....

....

....

....

....

....

....

....

....

....

....

....

....

....

....

TITLE

Author

Date   Recommended by

Opinions/Ideas

TITLE

Author

Date **Recommended by**

Opinions/Ideas

TITLE ....

Author ....

Date .... Recommended by ....

Opinions/Ideas ....

....

....

....

....

....

....

....

....

....

....

....

....

....

....

....

....

....

....

TITLE

Author

Date .... Recommended by

Opinions/Ideas

TITLE ....

Author ....

Date .... Recommended by ....

Opinions/Ideas ....

....

....

....

....

....

....

....

....

....

....

....

....

....

....

....

....

....

....

TITLE

Author

Date .... Recommended by

Opinions/Ideas

TITLE

Author

Date   Recommended by

Opinions/Ideas

TITLE

Author

Date   **Recommended by**

Opinions/Ideas

TITLE

Author

Date   Recommended by

Opinions/Ideas

TITLE...

Author...

Date........................ Recommended by..

Opinions/Ideas...

....

....

....

....

....

....

....

....

....

....

....

....

....

....

....

....

....

....

TITLE

Author

Date   Recommended by

Opinions/Ideas

TITLE ....

Author ....

Date .... Recommended by ....

Opinions/Ideas ....

....

....

....

....

....

....

....

....

....

....

....

....

....

....

....

....

....

TITLE ....

Author ....

Date .... Recommended by ....

Opinions/Ideas ....

....

....

....

....

....

....

....

....

....

....

....

....

....

....

....

....

....

....

....

TITLE

Author

Date   Recommended by

Opinions/Ideas

TITLE

Author

Date   Recommended by

Opinions/Ideas

TITLE ....

Author ....

Date .... **Recommended by** ....

Opinions/Ideas ....

....

....

....

....

....

....

....

....

....

....

....

....

....

....

....

....

....

....

TITLE

Author

Date   Recommended by

Opinions/Ideas

TITLE ....

Author ....

Date .... Recommended by ....

Opinions/Ideas ....

....

....

....

....

....

....

....

....

....

....

....

....

....

....

....

....

....

....

....

TITLE ....

Author ....

Date .... Recommended by ....

Opinions/Ideas ....

....

....

....

....

....

....

....

....

....

....

....

....

....

....

....

....

....

....

....

....

TITLE

Author

Date............................ Recommended by

Opinions/Ideas

.

TITLE

Author

Date .... **Recommended by**

Opinions/Ideas

TITLE ....

Author ....

Date .... **Recommended by** ....

Opinions/Ideas ....

....

....

....

....

....

....

....

....

....

....

....

....

....

....

....

....

....

....

TITLE

Author

Date   Recommended by

Opinions/Ideas

TITLE ....

Author ....

Date .... Recommended by ....

Opinions/Ideas ....

....

....

....

....

....

....

....

....

....

....

....

....

....

....

....

....

TITLE

Author

Date   Recommended by

Opinions/Ideas

TITLE

Author

Date Recommended by

Opinions/Ideas

TITLE ....

Author ....

Date .... Recommended by ....

Opinions/Ideas ....

....

....

....

....

....

....

....

....

....

....

....

....

....

....

....

....

....

....

TITLE ....

Author ....

Date .... Recommended by ....

Opinions/Ideas ....

....

....

....

....

....

....

....

....

....

....

....

....

....

....

....

....

....

TITLE

Author

Date .... **Recommended by** ....

Opinions/Ideas

TITLE..

Author...

Date........................ **Recommended by**............................

Opinions/Ideas..

....

....

....

....

....

....

....

....

....

....

....

....

....

....

....

....

....

....

....

TITLE

Author

Date   Recommended by

Opinions/Ideas

TITLE ....

Author ....

Date .... Recommended by ....

Opinions/Ideas ....

....

....

....

....

....

....

....

....

....

....

....

....

....

....

....

....

....

....

....

TITLE

Author

Date　　　　　　Recommended by

Opinions/Ideas

TITLE

Author

Date   Recommended by

Opinions/Ideas

TITLE

Author

Date   Recommended by

Opinions/Ideas

TITLE ....

Author ....

Date .... Recommended by ....

Opinions/Ideas ....

....

....

....

....

....

....

....

....

....

....

....

....

....

....

....

....

....

....

....

TITLE

Author

Date .... Recommended by

Opinions/Ideas

TITLE

Author

Date **Recommended by**

Opinions/Ideas

TITLE

Author

Date   Recommended by

Opinions/Ideas

Title

Author

Date   Recommended by

Opinions/Ideas

TITLE

Author

Date   Recommended by

Opinions/Ideas

TITLE ....

Author ....

Date .... Recommended by ....

Opinions/Ideas ....

....

....

....

....

....

....

....

....

....

....

....

....

....

....

....

....

....

TITLE

Author

Date   Recommended by

Opinions/Ideas

TITLE

Author

Date   Recommended by

Opinions/Ideas

TITLE..

Author ....

Date .... Recommended by..

Opinions/Ideas ....

....

....

....

....

....

....

....

....

....

....

....

....

....

....

....

....

....

TITLE ....

Author ....

Date .... **Recommended by** ....

Opinions/Ideas ....

....

....

....

....

....

....

....

....

....

....

....

....

....

....

....

....

....

....

....

....

TITLE

Author

Date   Recommended by

Opinions/Ideas

RECOMMENDED *Books and Audio Books*

TITLE

Author

Publisher

Recommended by

Notes

TITLE

Author

Publisher

Recommended by

Notes

TITLE

Author

Publisher

Recommended by

Notes

TITLE

Author

Publisher

Recommended by

Notes

TITLE

Author

Publisher

Recommended by

Notes

TITLE

Author

Publisher

Recommended by

Notes

TITLE

Author

Publisher

Recommended by

Notes

TITLE

Author

Publisher

Recommended by

Notes

TITLE

Author

Publisher

Recommended by

Notes

TITLE

Author

Publisher

Recommended by

Notes

TITLE

Author

Publisher

Recommended by

Notes

TITLE

Author

Publisher

Recommended by

Notes

TITLE ....

Author ....

Publisher ....

Recommended by ....

Notes ....

....

TITLE ....

Author ....

Publisher ....

Recommended by ....

Notes ....

....

TITLE ....

Author ....

Publisher ....

Recommended by ....

Notes ....

....

TITLE

Author

Publisher

Recommended by

Notes

TITLE

Author

Publisher

Recommended by

Notes

TITLE

Author

Publisher

Recommended by

Notes

TITLE ....

Author ....

Publisher ....

Recommended by ....

Notes ....

....

TITLE ....

Author ....

Publisher ....

Recommended by ....

Notes ....

....

TITLE ....

Author ....

Publisher ....

Recommended by ....

Notes ....

....

TITLE

Author

Publisher

Recommended by

Notes

TITLE

Author

Publisher

Recommended by

Notes

TITLE

Author

Publisher

Recommended by

Notes

TITLE

Author

Publisher

Recommended by

Notes

TITLE

Author

Publisher

Recommended by

Notes

TITLE

Author

Publisher

Recommended by

Notes

TITLE

Author

Publisher

Recommended by

Notes

TITLE

Author

Publisher

Recommended by

Notes

TITLE

Author

Publisher

Recommended by

Notes

TITLE

Author

Publisher

Recommended by

Notes

TITLE

Author

Publisher

Recommended by

Notes

TITLE

Author

Publisher

Recommended by

Notes

TITLE

Author

Publisher

Recommended by

Notes

TITLE

Author

Publisher

Recommended by

Notes

TITLE

Author

Publisher

Recommended by

Notes

TITLE

Author

Publisher

Recommended by

Notes

TITLE

Author

Publisher

Recommended by

Notes

TITLE

Author

Publisher

Recommended by

Notes

LOANED *Books and Audio Books*

TITLE

Author

Loaned to

Date Loaned

Date Returned

TITLE

Author

Loaned to

Date Loaned

Date Returned

TITLE

Author

Loaned to

Date Loaned

Date Returned

TITLE ....

Author ....

Loaned to ....

Date Loaned ....

Date Returned ....

TITLE ....

Author ....

Loaned to ....

Date Loaned ....

Date Returned ....

TITLE ....

Author ....

Loaned to ....

Date Loaned ....

Date Returned ....

TITLE

Author

Loaned to

Date Loaned

Date Returned

TITLE

Author

Loaned to

Date Loaned

Date Returned

TITLE

Author

Loaned to

Date Loaned

Date Returned

TITLE

Author

Loaned to

Date Loaned

Date Returned

TITLE

Author

Loaned to

Date Loaned

Date Returned

TITLE

Author

Loaned to

Date Loaned

Date Returned

TITLE

Author

Loaned to

Date Loaned

Date Returned

TITLE

Author

Loaned to

Date Loaned

Date Returned

TITLE

Author

Loaned to

Date Loaned

Date Returned

TITLE

Author

Loaned to

Date Loaned

Date Returned

TITLE

Author

Loaned to

Date Loaned

Date Returned

TITLE

Author

Loaned to

Date Loaned

Date Returned

TITLE ....

Author ....

Loaned to ....

Date Loaned ....

Date Returned ....

TITLE ....

Author ....

Loaned to ....

Date Loaned ....

Date Returned ....

TITLE ....

Author ....

Loaned to ....

Date Loaned ....

Date Returned ....

TITLE

Author

Loaned to

Date Loaned

Date Returned

TITLE

Author

Loaned to

Date Loaned

Date Returned

TITLE

Author

Loaned to

Date Loaned

Date Returned

TITLE

Author

Loaned to

Date Loaned

Date Returned

TITLE

Author

Loaned to

Date Loaned

Date Returned

TITLE

Author

Loaned to

Date Loaned

Date Returned

TITLE

Author

Loaned to

Date Loaned

Date Returned

TITLE

Author

Loaned to

Date Loaned

Date Returned

TITLE

Author

Loaned to

Date Loaned

Date Returned

TITLE

Author

Loaned to

Date Loaned

Date Returned

TITLE

Author

Loaned to

Date Loaned

Date Returned

TITLE

Author

Loaned to

Date Loaned

Date Returned

TITLE ....

Author ....

Loaned to ....

Date Loaned ....

Date Returned ....

TITLE ....

Author ....

Loaned to ....

Date Loaned ....

Date Returned ....

TITLE ....

Author ....

Loaned to ....

Date Loaned ....

Date Returned ....

TITLE

Author

Loaned to

Date Loaned

Date Returned

TITLE

Author

Loaned to

Date Loaned

Date Returned

TITLE

Author

Loaned to

Date Loaned

Date Returned

TITLE

Author

Loaned to

Date Loaned

Date Returned

TITLE

Author

Loaned to

Date Loaned

Date Returned

TITLE

Author

Loaned to

Date Loaned

Date Returned

TITLE

Author

Loaned to

Date Loaned

Date Returned

TITLE

Author

Loaned to

Date Loaned

Date Returned

TITLE

Author

Loaned to

Date Loaned

Date Returned

BORROWED *Books and Audio Books*

TITLE

Author

Borrowed From

Date Borrowed

Date Returned

TITLE

Author

Borrowed From

Date Borrowed

Date Returned

TITLE

Author

Borrowed From

Date Borrowed

Date Returned

TITLE

Author

Borrowed From

Date Borrowed

Date Returned

TITLE

Author

Borrowed From

Date Borrowed

Date Returned

TITLE

Author

Borrowed From

Date Borrowed

Date Returned

TITLE ....

Author ....

Borrowed From ....

Date Borrowed ....

Date Returned ....

TITLE ....

Author ....

Borrowed From ....

Date Borrowed ....

Date Returned ....

TITLE ....

Author ....

Borrowed From ....

Date Borrowed ....

Date Returned ....

TITLE ....

Author ....

Borrowed From ....

Date Borrowed ....

Date Returned ....

TITLE ....

Author ....

Borrowed From ....

Date Borrowed ....

Date Returned ....

TITLE ....

Author ....

Borrowed From ....

Date Borrowed ....

Date Returned ....

TITLE

Author

Borrowed From

Date Borrowed

Date Returned

TITLE

Author

Borrowed From

Date Borrowed

Date Returned

TITLE

Author

Borrowed From

Date Borrowed

Date Returned

TITLE ....

Author ....

Borrowed From ....

Date Borrowed ....

Date Returned ....

TITLE ....

Author ....

Borrowed From ....

Date Borrowed ....

Date Returned ....

TITLE ....

Author ....

Borrowed From ....

Date Borrowed ....

Date Returned ....

TITLE

Author

Borrowed From

Date Borrowed

Date Returned

TITLE

Author

Borrowed From

Date Borrowed

Date Returned

TITLE

Author

Borrowed From

Date Borrowed

Date Returned

TITLE

Author

Borrowed From

Date Borrowed

Date Returned

TITLE

Author

Borrowed From

Date Borrowed

Date Returned

TITLE

Author

Borrowed From

Date Borrowed

Date Returned

TITLE

Author

Borrowed From

Date Borrowed

Date Returned

TITLE

Author

Borrowed From

Date Borrowed

Date Returned

TITLE

Author

Borrowed From

Date Borrowed

Date Returned

TITLE ....

Author ....

Borrowed From ....

Date Borrowed ....

Date Returned ....

TITLE ....

Author ....

Borrowed From ....

Date Borrowed ....

Date Returned ....

TITLE ....

Author ....

Borrowed From ....

Date Borrowed ....

Date Returned ....

TITLE

Author

Borrowed From

Date Borrowed

Date Returned

TITLE

Author

Borrowed From

Date Borrowed

Date Returned

TITLE

Author

Borrowed From

Date Borrowed

Date Returned

TITLE

Author

Borrowed From

Date Borrowed

Date Returned

TITLE

Author

Borrowed From

Date Borrowed

Date Returned

TITLE

Author

Borrowed From

Date Borrowed

Date Returned

TITLE ....

Author ....

Borrowed From ....

Date Borrowed ....

Date Returned ....

TITLE ....

Author ....

Borrowed From ....

Date Borrowed ....

Date Returned ....

TITLE ....

Author ....

Borrowed From ....

Date Borrowed ....

Date Returned ....

TITLE ....

Author ....

Borrowed From ....

Date Borrowed ....

Date Returned ....

TITLE ....

Author ....

Borrowed From ....

Date Borrowed ....

Date Returned ....

TITLE ....

Author ....

Borrowed From ....

Date Borrowed ....

Date Returned ....

TITLE

Author

Borrowed From

Date Borrowed

Date Returned

TITLE

Author

Borrowed From

Date Borrowed

Date Returned

TITLE

Author

Borrowed From

Date Borrowed

Date Returned

Favorite PLACES *to Browse, Buy and Be With Books*

PLACE

Address

Telephone

Location Notes/Directions

Specialty/Notes

PLACE

Address

Telephone

Location Notes/Directions

Specialty/Notes

PLACE

Address

Telephone

Location Notes/Directions

Specialty/Notes

PLACE

Address

Telephone

Location Notes/Directions

Specialty/Notes

PLACE

Address

Telephone

Location Notes/Directions

Specialty/Notes

PLACE

Address

Telephone

Location Notes/Directions

Specialty/Notes

PLACE

Address

Telephone

Location Notes/Directions

Specialty/Notes

PLACE

Address

Telephone

Location Notes/Directions

Specialty/Notes

PLACE

Address

Telephone

Location Notes/Directions

Specialty/Notes

PLACE

Address

Telephone

Location Notes/Directions

Specialty/Notes

PLACE

Address

Telephone

Location Notes/Directions

Specialty/Notes

PLACE

Address

Telephone

Location Notes/Directions

Specialty/Notes

PLACE

Address

Telephone

Location Notes/Directions

Specialty/Notes

PLACE

Address

Telephone

Location Notes/Directions

Specialty/Notes

PLACE

Address

Telephone

Location Notes/Directions

Specialty/Notes

PLACE

Address

Telephone

Location Notes/Directions

Specialty/Notes

PLACE

Address

Telephone

Location Notes/Directions

Specialty/Notes

PLACE

Address

Telephone

Location Notes/Directions

Specialty/Notes

PLACE

Address

Telephone

Location Notes/Directions

Specialty/Notes

PLACE

Address

Telephone

Location Notes/Directions

Specialty/Notes

PLACE

Address

Telephone

Location Notes/Directions

Specialty/Notes

Your Own INDEX

TITLE	AUTHOR	PAGE

TITLE	AUTHOR	PAGE